Table of Contents

1 Understanding Your Tax Landscape

Navigating the tax system can feel like traversing a dense forest, especially for beginners. However, understanding the fundamentals is the first crucial step toward minimizing your tax burden. It's not about avoiding taxes altogether – that's illegal – but about legally reducing your tax liability through informed planning and strategic choices. This requires knowing the terrain, understanding the rules of the game, and utilizing the tools available to you. Remember, this isn't about finding "loopholes" in the strictest sense, but rather taking advantage of the legal allowances the tax system provides.

Federal income tax is a progressive tax system, meaning higher earners pay a larger percentage of their income in taxes. This is typically calculated based on your taxable income, which is your gross income less certain deductions and adjustments. State and local taxes vary widely; some states have no income tax, while others impose significant rates. Sales taxes, property taxes, and payroll taxes (including Social Security and Medicare taxes) further contribute to your overall tax liability. Understanding these different types of taxes is crucial to building a comprehensive tax strategy.

Many individuals make assumptions about the tax system that may not align with reality. For example, a common misconception is that all deductions are created equal. Itemized deductions, such as those for mortgage interest and charitable contributions, are different from standard deductions. It's often beneficial to compare which will lower your taxable income more, and it's crucial to determine what expenses qualify for each. Another myth? Thinking that only high-income earners need to worry about tax planning. Smart tax planning benefits everyone, regardless of income level. Effective strategies can significantly reduce your tax burden at any income level. Even seemingly small tax savings add up over time.

Knowing how to properly file your taxes is another crucial element. The IRS provides various forms and instructions; utilizing the correct form(s) is critical to avoiding penalties and delays. Accurate record-keeping is essential, not just for filing your tax return but also for potential audits. Retain all relevant documents—receipts, bank statements, investment records – for at least three years, preferably longer. This allows you to substantiate your tax claims in case of an audit. This diligent approach will minimize your stress and potential financial liability.

The complexity of tax laws is often overwhelming. However, seeking professional guidance can alleviate stress and ensure compliance. Enlisting the services of a qualified tax professional, such as a Certified Public Accountant (CPA), or a tax attorney can be invaluable. They can provide tailored advice based on your specific financial situation, helping you navigate complex regulations, and potentially saving you money in the long run. The cost of hiring a tax professional is often far outweighed by the potential savings they help you achieve. Remember, seeking expert advice is an investment, not an expense.

Finally, consider your long-term financial goals. Tax planning isn't just a yearly event; it's an ongoing process that should adapt with changes in your income, investments, and family situation. Regular review of your tax strategy, ideally annually, ensures that your plan aligns with your evolving circumstances and takes into account any changes in tax laws. Proactive planning enables you to take advantage of opportunities and avoid potential pitfalls. Making tax planning a regular habit builds a strong foundation for your financial future and ultimately, your financial freedom. It's about building a long-term strategy for financial success and not just reacting to immediate tax deadlines. This proactive approach will ultimately enhance your financial well-being.

1.1 Tax Basics

Understanding the basics of taxation is crucial for anyone seeking to minimize their tax burden. It's not about finding loopholes in the system—it's about understanding the rules and using them strategically. The first step is recognizing the different types of taxes you'll likely encounter. Federal income tax is a significant one, impacting most individuals and businesses. State income tax also applies in many states, adding another layer to your tax obligations. Sales tax, levied on purchases, is another common tax, varying in rates across different states and localities. Property taxes, assessed on real estate ownership, represent a recurring annual expense. Understanding these different tax types, their respective rates, and how they're calculated is fundamental to effective tax planning. Ignoring any of these aspects can lead to significant financial consequences. Remember, proactive engagement with the tax system is far more effective than reactive measures. Filing your taxes correctly is paramount. This involves accurate record-keeping, the diligent compilation of all relevant documentation, and choosing the appropriate tax form. Failing to file on time can result in penalties. It's also crucial to understand the difference between deductions and credits. Deductions lower your taxable income, while credits directly reduce your tax liability. Many people misunderstand this difference. For instance, a $1,000 deduction in a 25% tax bracket only saves $250, whereas a $1,000 tax credit saves $1,000 directly. Therefore, identifying and claiming available credits should be a priority. Knowing which

forms to use and the deadlines for filing is just as important; missing these can lead to unwanted penalties and interest charges.
Tax laws are complex and often change. Staying updated on these changes is essential, preventing costly mistakes. It's advisable to consult reliable sources, including the IRS website and reputable tax publications. Professional advice from a qualified tax advisor can prove invaluable. Their expertise can help navigate the complexities of tax law, ensuring compliance and identifying opportunities for tax optimization. Remember, seeking professional help is an investment in your financial well-being, especially when dealing with intricate aspects of tax planning, such as estate planning or investment strategies. While you may initially view the cost as an expense, the potential savings and avoidance of penalties significantly outweigh this cost.
Understanding your filing status significantly impacts your tax liability. This is determined by factors like marital status, dependents, and other qualifying circumstances. Choosing the incorrect filing status could lead to overpayment or underpayment of taxes. Accurate calculation of your income is also critical. This includes wages, salary, investment income, and any other source of revenue. Reporting this accurately is essential; failure to do so may lead to audits and penalties. Overlooking small details can accumulate, leading to significant errors in your overall tax assessment. This emphasizes the importance of diligent record-keeping and seeking professional guidance to ensure accuracy and compliance. Keep accurate records of all your transactions throughout the year. This makes tax preparation considerably easier and reduces the chances of mistakes.
Finally, remember that tax planning is an ongoing process. It's not something you do once and forget. Your financial circumstances change over time, requiring adjustments to your tax strategy. Regularly reviewing your tax situation, perhaps annually, helps you stay on top of things and take advantage of any changes that might benefit your situation. Your tax situation may evolve, requiring that you re-evaluate your approach to ensure ongoing compliance

and maximize tax advantages. This continuous process ensures your tax plan remains aligned with your financial goals and reflects any changes in tax laws. Proactive tax planning is crucial for long-term financial security and wealth building. By understanding tax basics and engaging in ongoing planning, you're better equipped to navigate the tax system effectively and minimize your tax burden legally.

1.2 Common Tax Myths

Many believe that filing taxes early guarantees a quicker refund. While it might seem logical, the truth is that the IRS processes returns based on receipt date and not filing date. Submitting your return early doesn't necessarily speed up the process; accuracy and completeness are far more critical. Focusing on error-free preparation will likely result in faster processing than simply rushing the submission.

The common misconception that all income is taxable is easily refuted. Numerous deductions and exclusions exist, legally reducing your taxable income. Understanding these provisions—retirement contributions, certain education expenses, and qualified health savings account (HSA) contributions—is key to minimizing your overall tax liability. Failing to leverage these reductions leaves money on the table, needlessly increasing your tax burden. Proactive research and thorough record-keeping are indispensable for identifying and utilizing every allowable deduction and exclusion.

Another persistent myth revolves around the idea that only high-income earners need to worry about tax planning. Effective tax planning benefits everyone, regardless of income level. Strategic planning can significantly lower your tax burden even on a modest income. Simple strategies like maximizing retirement contributions, understanding the standard deduction versus itemized deductions, and claiming all available credits can make a tangible difference, regardless of your salary bracket. Therefore, engaging in tax planning should be seen as a fundamental financial practice for all adults.

Many believe that hiring a tax professional automatically guarantees a lower tax bill. While professional advice is undeniably valuable, it's a tool, not a guarantee of reduced taxes. A tax professional's role is to help you navigate the complexities of the tax code and ensure you comply with all legal requirements, utilizing all available and legitimate strategies to reduce your tax liability. Ultimately, you are responsible for the accuracy of the information provided to the tax professional, and their work is based on the information you supply. A professional is, therefore, your partner in effective tax planning, not a magic bullet.

A surprisingly common misconception is that all tax deductions are created equal. They are not. Different deductions offer varying degrees of benefit and have specific eligibility criteria. It's crucial to understand the nuances of each deduction before claiming it. For instance, some deductions may be subject to limitations or phase-outs based on income. Careful assessment of each deduction's potential benefit relative to your unique financial circumstances is crucial for informed decision-making. Consulting tax guidance and resources available through reliable governmental and professional sources is strongly recommended to avoid errors.

Another prevalent myth is that only large corporations and wealthy individuals engage in tax planning. This simply isn't true. Tax planning is applicable to every individual and every entity that incurs a tax liability. From strategic use of tax-advantaged retirement accounts to understanding the implications of different business structures, tax planning is a tool available to everyone for financial well-being. Ignoring tax planning due to a perception of complexity or unavailability is a disservice to your own financial future.

It's often assumed that tax laws are static and unchanging. This is false. Tax laws regularly evolve, meaning what's relevant and beneficial today may not be so tomorrow. Regularly reviewing your tax strategies and adapting them to account for these legislative changes is crucial. Staying informed is essential to maintaining the effectiveness of your approach, ensuring you continue to leverage every available legal means of reducing your tax burden. Regularly reviewing tax law updates and considering professional consultation is a worthwhile investment in long-term financial security. The best way to stay informed is by subscribing to authoritative tax news publications or websites.

Finally, some believe that the tax system is inherently unfair and impossible to navigate. While the tax code may indeed be complicated, it isn't inherently unfair. It's a system with numerous provisions designed to support various financial circumstances and goals. With proper understanding and planning, the system can work to your advantage, minimizing your tax burden legally. The key is to obtain the necessary knowledge and utilize available resources such as reputable tax software or professionals, for effective and compliant tax planning. The aim is not to outsmart the system, but to work within its parameters to your greatest financial benefit.

2 Tax Deductions & Credits

The Internal Revenue Service (IRS) offers numerous deductions and credits designed to lessen your tax burden. Understanding the distinction is key; deductions reduce your taxable income, while credits directly reduce your tax liability. A deduction of $1,000, for instance, will save you $100 if you're in the 10% tax bracket, but $300 if you're in the 30% bracket. Credits, conversely, offer a dollar-for-dollar reduction, regardless of your tax bracket. A $1,000 credit saves you $1,000, period. This difference is significant in maximizing your tax savings.

Itemized deductions offer a pathway to potentially lower your taxable income. If your itemized deductions exceed the standard deduction amount, itemizing is advantageous. For example, mortgage interest, state and local taxes (subject to limitations), charitable contributions, and medical expenses exceeding a certain percentage of your adjusted gross income are all potentially deductible. Meticulous record-keeping is essential; you'll need documentation to substantiate each claim. Consult IRS Publication 503 for a comprehensive list of itemized deductions and their specific requirements. Remember, the goal is accuracy; the penalties for misrepresenting your deductions can outweigh any savings.

Tax credits, on the other hand, function as direct reductions in your tax liability. Several credits cater to specific circumstances. The Earned Income Tax Credit (EITC), for example, benefits low-to-moderate-income working individuals and families. The Child

Tax Credit (CTC) assists families with qualifying children. The American Opportunity Tax Credit (AOTC) and the Lifetime Learning Credit (LLC) help with higher education expenses. Eligibility criteria for each credit vary, so carefully review the IRS guidelines to determine your qualification and the amount you can claim. Don't overlook these valuable opportunities; they can significantly lower your tax bill, sometimes even resulting in a refund.

Claiming your deductions and credits requires careful preparation and accurate record-keeping. Begin by gathering all necessary documentation: W-2 forms, 1099 forms, receipts for charitable donations, medical bills, and any other relevant documents substantiating your claims. Organize your documents systematically, using a filing system that suits your preferences and ensures easy access to specific information when needed. Accuracy is paramount; even a small error can trigger an audit. Consider using tax preparation software or consulting a tax professional to ensure you're claiming all eligible deductions and credits. They can guide you through the process and help you avoid costly mistakes. Double-checking all your information before submitting your return is a vital step; you don't want to miss opportunities for savings due to oversights.

Beyond the standard deductions and credits, explore less commonly known possibilities. For homeowners, energy-efficient home improvements might qualify for tax credits. Depending on your location and circumstances, deductions for state and local taxes might apply. For those self-employed, home office deductions and other business-related expenses can significantly lower your taxable income. Thorough research is vital; familiarize yourself with the IRS publications relevant to your specific situation. Remember, utilizing these lesser-known deductions can dramatically affect your total tax liability. The IRS website is a wealth of information; it provides details on eligible expenses and the necessary documentation for each deduction and credit.

In conclusion, effectively utilizing tax deductions and credits is a crucial component of minimizing your tax burden. By understanding the distinctions between deductions and credits, meticulously maintaining records, and actively researching available options, you can significantly reduce your tax liability. Remember, a proactive approach is paramount. Don't wait until the last minute; allow ample time for gathering documents, researching eligibility, and preparing your return accurately. Proactive tax planning is an investment in your financial future. Through diligent planning, you can leverage these tools to achieve significant tax savings and enhance your overall financial well-being. Consider seeking professional guidance if you feel overwhelmed; tax professionals can provide expert advice and ensure compliance with all applicable tax laws and regulations.

2.1 Itemized Deductions

Itemizing deductions can significantly reduce your taxable income, a crucial aspect of minimizing your overall tax burden. Unlike the standard deduction, which provides a flat amount, itemizing allows you to deduct specific expenses, potentially leading to substantial savings. To effectively utilize itemized deductions, meticulous record-keeping is paramount; gather receipts, bank statements, and any other documentation that substantiates your claims. Failing to maintain organized records can result in rejected deductions, undermining your efforts and potentially leading to penalties. Accuracy and thoroughness are non-negotiable. Understanding which expenses qualify for itemization is critical. Medical expenses exceeding 7.5% of your adjusted gross income (AGI) are deductible, including doctor visits, prescription medications, and even certain long-term care costs. However, remember to carefully review IRS guidelines for detailed clarifications and restrictions. This seemingly simple deduction can add up significantly, particularly for individuals with significant healthcare expenses. Always double-check against the official IRS guidelines; their interpretations are binding.

State and local taxes (SALT) can also be itemized, subject to limitations established under the Tax Cuts and Jobs Act. This deduction includes property taxes, state income taxes, and sales taxes—however, there are annual limits; exceeding the cap renders further deduction ineligible. Carefully evaluate whether itemizing SALT offers a greater benefit than the standard deduction, a calculation that varies depending on your individual tax profile. A tax professional's insight can prove invaluable in making this assessment.

Home mortgage interest is another significant itemized deduction for homeowners. The interest paid on the first $750,000 of debt is typically deductible, but be aware of specific exceptions and regulations concerning second homes or home equity loans. Accurate calculation is essential; errors can have serious tax consequences. Keeping meticulous records of payments is essential to avoid mistakes and ensure you claim the full amount to which you are entitled.

Charitable contributions provide another avenue for reducing your tax liability. Donating to qualified charities entitles you to deduct the amount of your contribution, provided you maintain sufficient documentation. However, you must adhere to certain limitations; this deduction is not unlimited, and understanding these limits is crucial for maximizing its benefit. This includes meticulously recording each donation to ensure that you are claiming everything you are eligible for.

Casualty and theft losses can be itemized under certain circumstances. If you experience a significant loss due to a disaster or theft, you might be able to deduct the loss that exceeds 10% of your AGI after accounting for any insurance reimbursements. Ensure that you have documented proof of the loss, including police reports or insurance claim documentation; supporting evidence is vital for successful deduction claims. Thorough documentation is critical when claiming casualty losses to prevent your application from being denied.

Finally, remember that itemizing is only beneficial if the total of your itemized deductions surpasses the standard deduction amount. Carefully compare the two figures to determine the most advantageous strategy. You may find the standard deduction is a more straightforward and sometimes more lucrative option. Calculating both the itemized and standard deduction amounts is a crucial step in optimizing your tax strategy. This requires careful consideration and potentially the assistance of a tax professional. This chapter provides a comprehensive overview of itemized deductions; however, it's crucial to remember that tax laws are intricate and subject to change. Always consult with a qualified tax professional for personalized guidance that is both compliant and effective in minimizing your tax burden. Remember, the information provided here is for educational purposes only and does not constitute tax advice. Seeking professional advice ensures your strategies remain in line with current tax laws and optimally reduce your taxable income.

2.2 Tax Credits Explained

Tax credits, unlike deductions, directly reduce your tax liability, dollar for dollar. Understanding this fundamental difference is crucial for maximizing your tax savings. While a deduction lowers your taxable income, a credit lowers the actual amount of tax you owe. For example, a $1,000 deduction might save you $200 in taxes (at a 20% tax bracket), but a $1,000 credit saves you $1,000. This distinction is critical when strategizing your tax planning.
Many different types of tax credits exist, each with specific eligibility requirements and limitations. Researching available credits relevant to your personal circumstances is vital. For instance, the Earned Income Tax Credit (EITC) benefits low-to-moderate-income working individuals and families, offering a significant reduction in their tax burden. The Child Tax Credit (CTC) helps families with children, providing a credit for each qualifying child. These credits, along with others like the American Opportunity

Tax Credit (AOTC) for higher education expenses and the Child and Dependent Care Credit for childcare costs, can significantly impact your overall tax liability.

Navigating the complexities of tax credits requires meticulous attention to detail. Accurately completing the relevant tax forms is paramount; an error could lead to delays in receiving your refund or even penalties. The IRS provides comprehensive instructions for each credit, and taking the time to understand these instructions is essential. Don't hesitate to seek professional assistance if you find the process confusing—a tax professional can help you navigate the complexities and ensure you claim all the credits you're entitled to. Remember, the potential savings can be substantial.

Eligibility criteria for each tax credit often involve specific income limits, filing statuses, and qualifying expenses. For instance, the income limitations for the EITC are adjusted annually and vary based on filing status and the number of qualifying children. Similarly, the AOTC has both income and enrollment requirements. Before claiming any credit, carefully review the IRS publications pertaining to that specific credit to confirm your eligibility. These publications are available online and provide detailed explanations of the requirements and procedures for claiming each credit.

Beyond the readily available credits, consider exploring lesser-known credits which might apply to your situation. These could include credits for energy-efficient home improvements, adoption expenses, or medical expenses exceeding a certain percentage of your income. Investigating these niche credits could unearth significant tax savings you might have overlooked. Websites like the IRS website, and reputable financial planning resources, provide a comprehensive list of available credits and their associated eligibility criteria. Proactive research is key to maximizing your tax benefits.

Remember, accurately documenting all qualifying expenses is crucial for claiming tax credits. Keep detailed records of all receipts, invoices, and other supporting documentation. This documentation will be necessary should the IRS request verification of your claimed credits during an audit. Organizing your financial records efficiently, perhaps using a dedicated tax software program, will significantly streamline the process. Maintaining meticulous records is not only essential for successful claims but also for the overall integrity of your tax filings.

Claiming tax credits involves completing specific forms and schedules within your tax return. The forms vary depending on the type of credit you are claiming; for instance, Form 1040-NR is used by non-resident aliens. The instructions accompanying each form are vital in ensuring accurate completion. Reviewing the instructions carefully and seeking professional assistance if needed, will ensure compliance and prevent potential errors. Incorrectly completed forms can result in processing delays, or even worse, rejection of your claim.

Strategic tax planning should involve proactively identifying and utilizing all eligible tax credits. Incorporating this aspect into your overall financial strategy can result in significant long-term savings. Don't approach tax planning as a once-a-year event; rather, view it as an ongoing process requiring continuous evaluation and adjustment. This proactive approach ensures you maximize potential tax benefits throughout your financial life. Remember, the tax code is constantly evolving; staying informed about any changes is critical for maintaining optimal tax efficiency.

The benefits of understanding and effectively utilizing tax credits extend beyond immediate financial savings. Proper tax planning reduces overall tax liability, allowing for more disposable income, facilitating financial flexibility, and promoting financial security. This contributes positively to overall financial health and well-being. This translates to increased investment opportunities, debt reduction, and ultimately, greater financial independence. Taking the time and effort to thoroughly understand and utilize tax credits can be one of the most beneficial steps you take towards achieving long-term financial freedom.

2.3 Claiming Your Credits

The sheer number of available tax credits can feel overwhelming, a confusing maze of eligibility requirements and complex forms. Don't let this discourage you. Many credits are surprisingly straightforward to claim, and the potential savings are substantial, often exceeding the effort required. Begin by identifying your specific circumstances: are you a homeowner? Do you have dependents? What is your income level? These factors significantly influence the credits you can claim.

Focusing on credits for education is a smart starting point. The American Opportunity Tax Credit, for instance, offers significant relief for students pursuing higher education. Remember to keep meticulous records of all tuition payments, fees, and other qualified education expenses; these are crucial for accurate claim submissions. If you missed out on claiming this credit in previous years, don't despair – many credits can be claimed retrospectively, though it's advisable to consult a tax professional to ensure compliance. Careful planning ensures you don't overlook potential deductions or credits, maximizing your tax savings.

For those with dependents, the Child Tax Credit is a considerable advantage. This credit offers a substantial reduction in your tax liability for each qualifying child, providing relief to families and bolstering financial stability. The credit amount may vary depending on the child's age and your income, so reviewing the IRS guidelines is vital for an accurate calculation. Remember, accuracy is paramount. Inaccuracies in your claim, however unintentional, can lead to delays or even penalties. Double-check every figure, and consider using tax preparation software to minimize errors.

Beyond the familiar credits, explore lesser-known options, tailored to specific circumstances. These may include credits for energy-efficient home improvements, child and dependent care expenses, or adoption expenses. Depending on your location, state-specific credits might also be available, supplementing federal benefits. Thorough research is crucial; the IRS website is a valuable resource, offering detailed explanations and eligibility criteria for each available credit. Don't be afraid to seek professional guidance; a tax advisor can help navigate the intricacies of these less commonly discussed options.

While many credits have income limitations, don't automatically assume you're ineligible. Income thresholds are adjusted annually, and even if your income is near the limit, you might still qualify for a partial credit. Review the adjusted gross income (AGI) limits for each credit carefully. Many people mistakenly believe they are ineligible when, in fact, they might be entitled to at least a portion of the credit. This oversight can cost you significant savings. This is precisely why seeking professional help can be beneficial, allowing you to claim every credit you're lawfully entitled to.

Claiming your credits requires diligence and organization. Gather all necessary documentation well in advance of the tax filing deadline. This includes W-2 forms, 1099 forms, receipts for education expenses, medical bills, and any other supporting documents pertinent to the credits you intend to claim. A well-organized system for storing these documents will simplify the process and ensure you don't miss anything crucial, eliminating potential delays and complications during the filing process. Procrastination is your worst enemy in this realm; starting early ensures accuracy and minimizes stress.

Remember, accurately claiming your tax credits isn't merely about minimizing your tax burden; it's about optimizing your financial well-being. These credits represent a legitimate and often significant portion of your hard-earned income, money that should ideally stay in your possession to bolster your financial future. Claiming what's yours empowers your financial plan, providing more resources for investment, debt reduction, or simply enhancing your overall financial security. Don't view this as a complex, burdensome task, but as a crucial step in building a sound financial future. The effort you invest now will yield significant rewards for years to come. Embrace the opportunity; seize control of your finances.

3 Investment Strategies

Retirement planning is crucial for long-term financial security and tax benefits. Maximize contributions to tax-advantaged retirement accounts like 401(k)s and traditional IRAs, reducing your current taxable income. Remember, contributions to these accounts are often tax-deductible, directly lowering your tax liability for the current year. Carefully consider your income bracket and contribution limits; exceeding limits can result in penalties. For those with higher incomes, exploring Roth IRAs could be beneficial. Although contributions aren't tax-deductible, withdrawals in retirement are tax-free, a significant advantage in later years. Consider consulting with a financial advisor to determine the best strategy for your individual circumstances, factoring in your current and projected income, and your anticipated retirement lifestyle. Don't underestimate the power of consistent contributions – even small amounts over time can accumulate significantly due to compounding interest.

Tax-advantaged accounts provide significant opportunities to minimize your tax burden. Besides retirement accounts, explore options like health savings accounts (HSAs) if you have a high-deductible health plan. Contributions are tax-deductible, and the funds grow tax-free. Furthermore, withdrawals for qualified medical expenses are tax-free, offering triple tax advantages. Educational savings plans, such as 529 plans, provide tax benefits for college expenses. Contributions may not be deductible, but earnings grow tax-deferred, and withdrawals for qualified education expenses are tax-free. Understand the specific rules and regulations governing these accounts to maximize their tax benefits and avoid any penalties. Remember, each account has its own set of contribution limits and withdrawal rules, so thorough research is essential before investing. Seeking professional guidance ensures you align your choices with your individual financial goals and tax situation.

Real estate investments offer various tax advantages. Depreciation deductions allow you to deduct a portion of your property's value each year, reducing your taxable income. This deduction is particularly valuable for rental properties. Mortgage interest is also deductible, further lowering your tax liability. Capital gains taxes on the sale of a property can be deferred or minimized through strategic tax planning, like a 1031 exchange. This allows you to reinvest your profits into another like-kind property without paying taxes immediately. However, navigating the complexities of real estate investing requires careful planning and understanding of tax implications. Consult with a real estate professional and a tax advisor to make informed decisions and take full advantage of the tax benefits available while mitigating risks effectively. Thorough due diligence is crucial before any real estate investment, considering factors like property value, rental income potential, and potential maintenance costs.

Diversification is key to mitigating risk and optimizing tax efficiency. Spread your investments across different asset classes, such as stocks, bonds, real estate, and commodities, to reduce the impact of any single investment's underperformance. Consider tax-efficient investments like municipal bonds, which are generally exempt from federal income tax. However, remember that diversification doesn't eliminate risk entirely, and some investments might be more suitable depending on your risk tolerance and investment horizon. The strategy to achieve a well-diversified portfolio needs to consider factors such as asset allocation, risk tolerance and investment time horizon. Regular review and adjust-

ment to your investment portfolio is necessary to keep up with the dynamic market landscape. Seeking professional advice to create a suitable diversification strategy is always recommended.
Effective risk management is essential to protect your investments and minimize potential tax liabilities. Diversification is a crucial aspect of risk management, but it's not the only one. Consider hedging strategies to mitigate potential losses. Insurance policies, such as property insurance for real estate investments, can protect against unforeseen events. Proper record-keeping is essential to support tax deductions and credits if audited. Maintain accurate records of all transactions, including receipts and supporting documentation. This helps avoid penalties related to inaccurate reporting. Consulting a tax professional can help create a comprehensive risk management strategy tailored to your specific circumstances. They can help you identify and mitigate potential risks, ensuring your investments are protected and tax-efficient. Remember, a proactive approach to risk management will limit future problems and save you both money and stress.

3.1 Retirement Planning

Retirement planning is crucial for long-term financial security, especially when considering tax implications. Many people mistakenly believe that retirement savings are untouched by taxes, leading to poor planning and unexpected tax burdens later in life. Understanding the tax advantages and disadvantages of different retirement accounts is paramount to maximizing your savings and minimizing your tax liability throughout your retirement years. Careful planning now can significantly impact your financial well-being during retirement.
One of the most common retirement savings vehicles is the 401(k) plan. Contributions made to a 401(k) are typically tax-deferred, meaning that you don't pay taxes on the money until you withdraw it in retirement. However, your employer's matching con-

tributions are usually taxed as income in the year received. This allows your money to grow tax-free until retirement, potentially leading to a significantly larger nest egg. However, withdrawals in retirement are taxed as ordinary income, a point many overlook during their working years. It's vital to plan for this taxation and adjust your withdrawal strategy accordingly. Understanding the nuances of your specific 401(k) plan is therefore critical.

Traditional Individual Retirement Accounts (IRAs) offer similar tax advantages to 401(k)s. Contributions to a traditional IRA may be tax-deductible, reducing your taxable income in the year of contribution. As with 401(k)s, the earnings grow tax-deferred, and withdrawals in retirement are taxed as ordinary income. The annual contribution limits are lower than for 401(k)s, but IRAs provide greater flexibility. However, it's important to note that IRA contributions aren't always fully deductible, depending on income and participation in employer-sponsored retirement plans. Knowing these nuances is essential for proper IRA planning.

Roth IRAs offer a contrasting approach to retirement savings. Contributions to a Roth IRA are made after tax, meaning you pay taxes on the money now. However, withdrawals in retirement are tax-free, a significant advantage. This can be particularly beneficial if you anticipate being in a higher tax bracket during retirement than you are currently. However, the upfront tax payment might seem less appealing to individuals with lower incomes or higher tax burdens currently. The decision to use a Roth IRA depends entirely on an individual's specific circumstances and long-term financial projections. Careful tax projections are necessary to make the optimal decision.

Beyond these specific accounts, various other investment strategies can play a role in your retirement tax planning. For example, investing in tax-efficient mutual funds or exchange-traded funds (ETFs) can reduce your overall tax burden throughout your savings period and even in retirement. These funds often employ strategies that minimize capital gains distributions, benefiting long-term investors. Remember, always consult a qualified financial advisor to find the strategies which most benefit your tax situation.

Real estate investment provides another avenue for retirement tax planning. While some strategies offer significant tax advantages, such as depreciation deductions, others can create tax liabilities that may outweigh those benefits. Holding a property for a considerable period can offer significant long-term tax benefits but requires careful planning to mitigate short-term losses and ensure your tax obligations are managed efficiently. Each individual's circumstance will dictate the potential success or potential pitfalls of real estate investment, therefore it's essential to consult an expert in real estate before making any significant investment.

Finally, consider the impact of inflation and potential tax law changes on your retirement plan. Regularly reviewing and adjusting your strategy is crucial, particularly concerning inflation's eroding effect on your savings. Taxes can change drastically throughout your lifetime. Therefore, it's wise to stay informed of tax policy changes and adapt your investments appropriately. Professional guidance will greatly enhance your preparation, ensuring that your retirement plan remains effective despite the inevitability of future tax policy changes.

Careful planning and a thorough understanding of tax laws are critical to maximizing your retirement savings and minimizing your tax liability. This might include working with a financial advisor and tax professional to develop a strategy tailored to your individual circumstances. This is the most effective way to guarantee an income sufficient for your retirement. Don't delay; start planning for a financially secure retirement today. A well-structured retirement plan, coupled with informed tax strategies, can significantly improve your overall financial well-being in your later years. Take control of your financial future now to maximize benefits during and after your retirement years.

3.2 Tax-Advantaged Accounts

Tax-advantaged accounts offer significant benefits for long-term financial growth while simultaneously reducing your tax burden. Understanding the nuances of these accounts is crucial for maximizing your savings and minimizing your tax liability. Different accounts cater to various financial goals and risk tolerances, so careful consideration is vital before making any investment decisions.

The most common tax-advantaged accounts are retirement accounts, such as 401(k)s and IRAs. 401(k) plans are employer-sponsored retirement savings plans that often include employer matching contributions, effectively increasing your savings. Contributions to 401(k)s are typically pre-tax, meaning you reduce your taxable income in the present year. However, withdrawals in retirement are taxed as ordinary income.

Individual Retirement Accounts (IRAs) provide another avenue for tax-advantaged retirement savings. Traditional IRAs offer similar pre-tax contributions and tax-deferred growth to 401(k)s, but with higher contribution limits for many. Conversely, Roth IRAs involve contributions made with after-tax dollars, but withdrawals in retirement are tax-free, a significant advantage for those anticipating a higher tax bracket in retirement. The choice between a traditional and Roth IRA depends largely on your current and projected tax brackets.

Beyond retirement accounts, other tax-advantaged accounts exist, offering unique benefits. Health Savings Accounts (HSAs) are designed specifically for individuals enrolled in high-deductible health plans. Contributions to HSAs are tax-deductible, the funds grow tax-free, and withdrawals for qualified medical expenses are tax-free. This trifecta of tax advantages makes HSAs a powerful tool for managing healthcare costs.

529 plans are another option, specifically designed to fund education expenses. Contributions to 529 plans are not tax-deductible

at the federal level, though some states offer state tax deductions. However, the earnings grow tax-free, and withdrawals are tax-free if used for qualified education expenses. This makes them a valuable tool for families planning for future college or higher education costs.

Choosing the right tax-advantaged account requires careful consideration of your individual circumstances, financial goals, and risk tolerance. For example, if you anticipate being in a higher tax bracket in retirement, a Roth IRA might be a better choice than a traditional IRA. Similarly, if you're planning for a child's college education, a 529 plan offers substantial tax benefits. Remember, understanding your personal financial situation is paramount.

While tax advantages are a significant benefit, it's crucial to remember the rules and regulations associated with each account. Contribution limits, withdrawal penalties, and eligibility criteria vary, so thorough research is crucial before making any investment decisions. Consulting with a qualified financial advisor can provide personalized guidance based on your unique circumstances, leading you toward the best tax strategy. They can help navigate the complexities of these plans, ensuring you make the best choices for your long-term financial well-being.

Careful planning is essential to effectively utilize tax-advantaged accounts. It's not merely about choosing the right account; it's about integrating it into a broader financial strategy. This comprehensive strategy should align with your personal financial goals – whether it's retirement planning, funding education, or simply maximizing tax savings. Regularly reviewing and adjusting your investment strategy is vital to ensure it remains effective and efficient.

Moreover, staying informed about potential changes in tax laws is crucial. Tax laws are dynamic and change periodically, potentially impacting the benefits of various accounts. Staying abreast of these changes ensures your financial plan remains optimal and complies with current regulations. Utilizing reputable financial resources and consulting experts ensures you adapt your strategy

accordingly, preserving the tax advantages and safeguarding your financial future.
Remember, this information is for educational purposes and not financial advice. Consult with a qualified financial advisor to determine the best course of action for your specific financial situation. They can provide personalized guidance tailored to your individual needs and help you navigate the complexities of tax-advantaged accounts to maximize their benefits. The goal is to achieve tax freedom, not merely to understand the mechanics of tax-advantaged accounts. A thorough understanding, combined with professional guidance, will pave the way toward a secure and prosperous financial future.

3.3 Real Estate Investments

Real estate investment offers significant tax advantages, particularly for those seeking to minimize their overall tax burden. Understanding these advantages requires careful planning and a grasp of specific tax deductions and credits available to property owners. One key area to focus on is depreciation. Depreciation allows you to deduct a portion of your property's value each year, reducing your taxable income. This is a powerful tool for reducing your tax liability, particularly in the early years of ownership when depreciation is highest. Remember to consult with a tax professional to determine the appropriate depreciation method and schedule for your specific situation, ensuring you're claiming the maximum allowable deduction without triggering any audits. Accurate record-keeping is crucial; maintain detailed records of all expenses related to the property, from mortgage interest payments to property taxes and maintenance costs.
Beyond depreciation, various other deductions can substantially lower your tax liability. For instance, mortgage interest is often a significant deduction. While the specifics can vary based on your mortgage type and the year you purchased the property, under-

standing the rules surrounding mortgage interest deductions is crucial. Additionally, property taxes are generally deductible, reducing your taxable income. This can represent a considerable savings, especially for properties in areas with high property tax rates. Always keep meticulous records of these payments, organizing them in a manner suitable for a potential tax audit. You should ensure that everything is perfectly up to date to avoid any complications or penalties.

Capital gains taxes are a significant consideration when selling investment properties. However, there are strategies to mitigate these taxes. One method is through the 1031 exchange, which allows you to defer capital gains taxes by reinvesting the proceeds from the sale of one property into another like-kind property. Understanding the rules and regulations governing 1031 exchanges is critical. It's essential to work with experienced real estate and tax professionals to ensure compliance with these complex regulations. The process requires careful timing and precise execution to avoid unforeseen complications or penalties. Thorough due diligence, including a complete understanding of the tax implications of every action, is paramount.

Passive activity losses, often incurred from rental properties, present unique tax challenges. Passive activity loss rules limit the amount of losses you can deduct against other income, specifically ordinary income, and you must have material participation in the real estate investment. However, savvy planning can help you manage these losses effectively. This might involve carefully structuring your investments to offset passive losses with passive income or employing strategies to increase your active participation in the property. Consulting with a tax professional is vital to developing a comprehensive strategy to address the particular challenges of passive activity losses.

Beyond individual tax deductions, certain tax credits can also provide relief. While less common than deductions, understanding these credits is essential for minimizing your overall tax burden. Research local and state tax incentives, as some areas offer special credits for investing in properties within designated zones or for making specific property improvements. Remember to stay informed about any changes in tax laws and regulations, as eligibility criteria and credit amounts can shift over time. Proactive tax planning is crucial, requiring constant monitoring of any relevant changes, so that your tax strategy remains compliant and effective. You should always be aware of the legislation and the possible modifications.

The selection of a suitable business structure is a crucial element in optimizing the tax efficiency of your real estate investments. Depending on your situation and the scale of your operations, a limited liability company (LLC), a partnership, or other structures may offer superior tax benefits compared to a sole proprietorship. It is important to carefully evaluate the implications of each structure on your tax liability, factoring in the complexities of state and local regulations. Consult with a tax professional or accountant experienced in real estate and business taxation to make an informed decision aligned with your financial and risk tolerance profile. Remember, the right structure can make a significant difference in the long-run efficiency of your tax situation.

Effective record-keeping is paramount throughout the entire process of real estate investment. Maintain detailed and organized records of all transactions, expenses, and income. This meticulous record-keeping is not only crucial for accurately calculating your tax liability but also serves as a strong defense in case of a tax audit. Adopt a robust system for storing and managing your financial documents, ensuring easy access and retrieval when necessary. Digital solutions and well-organized filing systems can significantly streamline this process, ensuring compliance and facilitating swift responses to any potential tax inquiries. Proactive organization is far easier to manage than reactive scrambling for information during tax season. Always stay organized!

3.4 Diversification Strategies

A diversified investment portfolio is more than just a collection of assets; it's a strategic approach to mitigating risk and maximizing returns, especially crucial when considering your overall tax situation. Remember, the goal isn't merely to accumulate wealth, but to accumulate wealth efficiently, minimizing your tax burden along the way. This necessitates a keen understanding of how different asset classes interact with the tax code, and how their performance can influence your overall tax liability.

Investing solely in one asset class, such as stocks, exposes you to significant market fluctuations and potential tax implications. A sudden drop in the stock market might trigger capital gains taxes on any sales made, even if you're aiming for long-term growth. Conversely, overreliance on a single low-risk investment could mean slower growth and missed opportunities for tax-advantaged gains. The ideal scenario, therefore, involves spreading your investments across a variety of asset classes, each with its own risk profile and tax characteristics.

Consider incorporating real estate into your portfolio. Real estate can offer tax benefits like depreciation deductions, which can significantly reduce your taxable income. However, it's essential to understand the nuances of real estate taxation, including capital gains taxes on the sale of properties, property taxes, and potential depreciation recapture. Careful planning and consultation with a tax advisor are crucial to maximize these benefits while mitigating potential tax liabilities.

Tax-advantaged retirement accounts, like 401(k)s and Roth IRAs, play a pivotal role in long-term tax planning. While contributions to traditional 401(k)s reduce your current taxable income, withdrawals in retirement are taxed as ordinary income. Conversely, Roth IRAs involve contributing after-tax dollars, but withdrawals in retirement are tax-free. The best choice depends on your individual circumstances, anticipated tax bracket in retirement, and long-term financial goals. Don't underestimate the power of these vehicles; they're designed to work in harmony with your overall tax strategy.

Diversification extends beyond simply choosing different asset classes; it also involves geographical diversification. Investing in international markets can offer exposure to different economies and currency fluctuations, potentially reducing overall portfolio risk. However, international investments might come with more complex tax reporting requirements and potential foreign tax credits to consider. Understanding the tax implications of international investments is vital for successful long-term planning.

Remember, diversification isn't a one-time decision; it's an ongoing process. Your financial situation and investment goals change over time, so you should regularly review your portfolio and make adjustments as necessary. Market conditions, tax laws, and personal circumstances all influence your optimal level of diversification. A periodic evaluation, perhaps annually, ensures your portfolio remains aligned with your evolving needs and tax objectives.

It's highly recommended to seek professional financial and tax advice when implementing a diversification strategy. A qualified financial advisor can help you create a personalized portfolio that aligns with your risk tolerance, financial goals, and overall tax strategy. They can also provide insights into the tax implications of your investment choices, assisting you in navigating the complexities of the tax code. Remember that proactive tax planning is not just about minimizing taxes today, it's about securing a financially secure and tax-efficient future. This holistic approach protects your hard-earned money and allows you to focus on the things that truly matter. Ignoring the interplay of tax laws and investment strategies can lead to unforeseen financial consequences, so remember, informed decisions always lead to better outcomes. This collaborative approach empowers you to take control of your financial destiny and chart a course towards financial freedom. Never underestimate the value of seeking expertise; doing so can significantly enhance your long-term success. The benefits of proper diversification, guided by professionals, far outweigh the potential costs. By actively managing your portfolio and staying informed about tax law changes, you'll be well-positioned to navigate the complexities of the financial landscape and achieve your long-term financial goals. This comprehensive strategy ensures you not only build wealth but also protect it. Remember, investing is a marathon, not a sprint. With careful planning and consistent effort, you can secure a prosperous and tax-efficient future.

3.5 Risk Management

Effective risk management is crucial for preserving your financial well-being, especially when employing aggressive tax-minimization strategies. While legal loopholes offer significant advantages, they often involve a degree of inherent risk. Understanding and mitigating these risks is not optional; it's fundamental to safeguarding your hard-earned savings and avoiding potentially devastating financial consequences. Proactive risk management isn't just about avoiding problems; it's about strategically positioning yourself for long-term financial success.

Many aggressive tax strategies, while perfectly legal, rely on specific interpretations of tax law, which can be subject to change. A shift in legislation or a reassessment by the IRS could significantly alter your tax liability, potentially resulting in unexpected tax bills, penalties, and interest. Therefore, staying informed about changes in tax law is paramount. Regularly review relevant publications and seek professional advice to ensure your strategies remain compliant. Don't underestimate the power of knowledge in this arena.

Diversification plays a vital role in managing investment risk. Don't put all your eggs in one basket, especially when using investments to reduce your tax burden. A diversified portfolio reduces your exposure to individual investment failures. Consider spreading your investments across various asset classes like

stocks, bonds, real estate, and commodities. This approach mitigates the impact of poor performance in any single sector, protecting your overall financial position. Remember that a well-diversified portfolio is a cornerstone of sound financial planning.
Maintaining meticulous records is not simply a matter of compliance; it's a critical risk management tool. Accurate and organized financial records provide the necessary documentation to substantiate your tax claims in case of an audit. Failing to keep proper records can severely weaken your position during an audit and lead to increased tax liability or penalties. This is an area where precision is non-negotiable. Consider using accounting software, working with a tax professional, or implementing a detailed filing system to guarantee accurate documentation.
The selection of tax professionals is also a significant risk management decision. Choosing a competent and ethical advisor with expertise in tax law is paramount. A poorly chosen advisor could lead to incorrect tax filings, increased liabilities, and even legal repercussions. Therefore, always thoroughly vet potential advisors, checking references, confirming their qualifications, and ensuring they have a clean professional record before entrusting them with your financial well-being. This seemingly small step can prevent significant future problems.
Beyond professional advice, it's vital to understand the limits of your own knowledge. While learning about tax law can be empowering, it's important to recognize when you need expert help. Complex situations require professional guidance, especially when considering intricate tax-minimization strategies. Trying to handle everything yourself can lead to costly mistakes. Understanding your limitations and seeking professional help when necessary is a hallmark of responsible risk management. Think of it as an investment in your financial security.
Consider the implications of unforeseen circumstances. Life events such as job loss, unexpected medical expenses, or market downturns can dramatically affect your financial planning. A comprehensive risk management plan should anticipate such

situations and incorporate strategies to mitigate their impact on your tax position. Having an emergency fund, a robust financial plan, and flexible strategies can help you weather unexpected storms. This is where truly long-term planning shows its value.

Regularly reviewing your tax strategy is a proactive step that allows for adjustments based on changes in your financial situation, tax law, or market conditions. Annual reviews, or even more frequent checks depending on the complexity of your situation, are crucial for identifying and addressing potential risks before they become significant problems. This is an ongoing process that ensures your strategies remain relevant and effective. This ongoing assessment is more than just maintenance; it's an act of intelligent risk management.

In conclusion, risk management is an integral aspect of tax optimization. It's not about eliminating risk entirely—that's often impossible—but about understanding, mitigating, and strategically preparing for potential problems. By combining thorough research, sound professional advice, meticulous record-keeping, and regular reviews, you can significantly reduce your tax-related risks and ensure the long-term success of your tax-minimization strategies. Remember, this is a journey, not a destination. Continuous vigilance and adaptation are key to navigating the complexities of the tax landscape and achieving lasting tax freedom.

4 Business Tax Optimization

Choosing the right business structure is paramount. A sole proprietorship offers simplicity, blending your personal and business finances, but this lacks liability protection and often results in higher personal tax rates. Conversely, an LLC (Limited Liability Company) provides a crucial separation of personal and business assets, shielding personal wealth from business debts, while offering flexible tax options, such as being taxed as a sole proprietorship, partnership, or even a corporation, depending on your state's regulations and your specific needs. Corporations, while offering the strongest liability protection, face more complex regulations and potentially higher tax burdens due to double taxation on profits. Carefully weigh the advantages and disadvantages of each structure considering your current financial situation, risk tolerance, and long-term business goals. Consult with both a tax professional and a legal advisor to make the most informed decision for your unique circumstances, as the best choice will depend entirely on the specifics of your business and your individual situation.

Effective expense management is crucial for minimizing your tax burden. Meticulously track all business expenses, ensuring you keep detailed records, including receipts, invoices, and bank statements. Categorize expenses according to the IRS guidelines

to ensure you only claim legitimate business deductions. Understand the difference between ordinary and necessary business expenses; ordinary expenses are common in your business type, while necessary expenses are helpful for your operations. Utilize accounting software to streamline this process; many programs automate expense tracking and reporting, reducing the chances of errors and omissions. Regularly reconcile your accounts to identify and correct any discrepancies promptly. Don't underestimate the importance of organizing your financial records; having a solid system will save you time and money, reducing the likelihood of facing an audit or incurring penalties. Aim for a systematic approach to record-keeping, enabling efficient tax preparation and minimizing the stress associated with filing.
Maximize allowable deductions to reduce your taxable income. Familiarize yourself with the wide range of deductible business expenses, such as rent, utilities, office supplies, employee wages, professional fees, and travel costs. Remember, home office deductions require a dedicated and exclusively used workspace, and accurate record-keeping is crucial for substantiating these claims. For vehicle expenses, maintain detailed logs of business mileage to calculate the deductible amount accurately. Remember, the IRS scrutinizes deductions; accurate documentation is vital to support your claims. Don't hesitate to consult with a tax professional for guidance on less common, potentially deductible expenses, as they may possess specialized knowledge of relevant tax laws that may not be immediately evident. The goal is to utilize all lawful avenues to minimize your taxable income while upholding complete compliance with tax regulations.
Beyond routine expenses, explore potential tax credits that can significantly reduce your tax liability. The research and development (R&D) tax credit incentivizes innovation by offering tax breaks for companies investing in new technologies or processes. The work opportunity tax credit rewards businesses for hiring individuals from specific disadvantaged groups. Eligibility criteria vary, so carefully review the IRS guidelines to determine your po-

tential qualification. Understanding and applying for applicable tax credits could save a considerable amount. These credits are often underutilized, but they present substantial opportunities for significant tax savings; therefore, proactive investigation is key. Do not hesitate to consult a qualified tax professional; these specialists can analyze your specific circumstances, determine your eligibility for any applicable credits, and help you navigate the often complex application process.

Strategic planning extends beyond current expenses; proactively adapt to future tax law changes. Stay informed about potential tax reform through reputable sources like the IRS website and professional tax publications. Attend tax seminars, webinars, or workshops to gain insights from tax experts and anticipate future adjustments to your tax strategy. Engage in continuous learning to ensure your business maintains compliance and adapts to changing tax laws effectively. Remember, proactive adaptation minimizes the risk of unexpected tax liabilities. By staying informed, you can make informed decisions, protecting your business from potential pitfalls associated with sudden legislative shifts. Incorporate tax planning into your overall business strategy. View tax optimization not merely as a compliance issue but as a strategic aspect of long-term business growth and sustainability.

4.1 Business Structures

Choosing the right business structure is paramount for tax optimization. The structure you select significantly impacts your personal liability, administrative burden, and, crucially, your tax obligations. A sole proprietorship, the simplest form, blends your business and personal finances, making you personally liable for all business debts and taxes. This simplicity comes at a cost; your personal income is directly taxed, offering fewer avenues for tax reduction compared to other structures. Understanding this trade-off is key to making an informed decision. Consider your risk tolerance and the complexity you're willing to manage.

A partnership, involving two or more individuals, offers some benefits but also shares the unlimited liability aspect of a sole proprietorship. Profit and losses are divided according to the partnership agreement, and each partner reports their share on their individual tax returns. While this structure can offer some tax advantages through deductions and credits shared amongst partners, careful planning and a well-defined agreement are essential to avoid future disputes and unforeseen tax liabilities. Seek professional advice to navigate the intricacies of partnership agreements and tax implications.

Limited Liability Companies (LLCs) have become incredibly popular due to their flexibility and limited liability protection. LLCs separate your personal assets from business liabilities, shielding your personal wealth from business debts. The tax treatment of an LLC can vary; it can be taxed as a sole proprietorship, partnership, S corporation, or even a C corporation, depending on your election and state regulations. This flexibility allows you to choose the structure that best minimizes your tax burden, but it requires careful consideration of the specific tax implications of each option. The choice is not trivial. Consulting with a tax professional is essential to navigate the complexities and make an informed decision.

S corporations provide a pathway to separate your personal income from your business income, thereby potentially lowering your overall tax liability. While the business itself doesn't pay corporate income tax, profits and losses are passed through directly to the shareholders, who report them on their individual tax returns. This structure can be beneficial if you anticipate a significant amount of income, as it might allow you to pay lower self-employment taxes than under other structures. However, S corporations also come with increased administrative requirements and compliance costs, including more stringent bookkeeping and record-keeping obligations. It is important to assess if the potential tax savings outweigh the increased complexity and potential

administrative burden.
C corporations are separate legal entities, distinct from their owners. This structure offers the strongest liability protection but also incurs double taxation—the corporation pays taxes on its profits, and shareholders pay taxes on their dividends. While this might seem disadvantageous, C corporations can be beneficial for larger businesses with significant profits, particularly those planning for substantial growth and future capital investment. The ability to raise capital through stock sales and to deduct various corporate expenses can offset some of the tax burden. It's advisable to weigh these advantages against the higher administrative costs and tax complexities associated with C-corporations. This consideration is vital for long-term financial health.
The optimal choice depends significantly on individual circumstances, including income levels, anticipated expenses, risk tolerance, and long-term business goals. The complexity of tax laws requires thorough consideration and the guidance of qualified professionals. A well-informed decision regarding your business structure is not only crucial for minimizing your tax liability in the present but also for long-term financial security and sustainable growth. Failing to select the appropriate structure can lead to increased tax burdens and significant legal complications down the line. This is a decision that demands due diligence and professional counsel. Remember that tax laws are subject to change, so regular review and adjustments are key to preserving your tax-efficient strategy over time. Therefore, the initial choice is merely the beginning of an ongoing process of adaptation and optimization. Proactive management of your business structure will safeguard your financial future and minimize your tax burden effectively. You need to take action promptly.

4.2 Expense Management

Effective expense management is crucial for minimizing your tax burden, especially for business owners. Properly categorizing and documenting your expenses can significantly reduce your taxable income. Remember, the IRS scrutinizes expense claims; therefore, meticulous record-keeping is paramount. Retain all receipts, invoices, and bank statements, organizing them methodically for easy access during tax season or potential audits. This diligent approach not only safeguards you from penalties but also demonstrates your commitment to tax compliance, projecting an image of financial responsibility to any auditing agency.

Understanding which expenses are deductible is vital. While the specifics vary depending on your business structure and industry, some common deductible expenses include rent or mortgage interest on business property, utilities, supplies, employee wages, professional services (like accounting or legal fees), and marketing or advertising costs. However, it's imperative to understand the nuances of each deduction. For instance, home office deductions require careful adherence to IRS guidelines to prove the exclusive and regular use of a portion of your home for business purposes. Similarly, vehicle expenses need detailed logging of business mileage versus personal use. Ignoring these specifics can lead to disallowed deductions and potential penalties. Always consult with a tax professional to ensure you're correctly applying deductions and avoiding pitfalls.

Beyond simply identifying deductible expenses, optimizing their impact on your tax liability requires strategic planning. Consider bundling expenses to maximize deductions. For example, instead of making many small purchases, strategically group similar items to create larger, more impactful deductions. This careful approach can enhance your overall tax savings and improve the overall efficiency of your deductions. This method presents a clearer picture of your spending habits, allowing for better financial management and more efficient tax preparation.

Don't underestimate the importance of separating business and personal expenses meticulously. Commingling funds can blur the lines, making it difficult to determine which expenses are legitimately deductible. This not only increases the risk of an audit but could also result in significant penalties if the IRS detects any inconsistencies. Maintain separate bank accounts and credit cards for business transactions, ensuring clear separation and ease of tracking expenditures. This diligent approach simplifies the record-keeping process, making tax preparation considerably easier and less stressful. Furthermore, this separation strengthens your claim for legitimacy when you file your taxes.

Technology plays an increasingly vital role in efficient expense management. Numerous accounting software programs and apps automate expense tracking, categorize transactions, and generate reports for tax preparation. These tools greatly simplify the process, reducing the risk of errors and improving overall accuracy. Some platforms even integrate directly with your bank accounts and credit cards, automatically categorizing expenses and generating financial reports. Choosing the right software depends on your business needs and complexity, but the potential time savings and increased accuracy are undeniable. Implementing such technologies reduces the likelihood of inconsistencies and makes the tax filing process streamlined.

Finally, remember that expense management isn't a one-time task; it's an ongoing process. Regularly review your expenses, compare them to previous periods, and analyze trends. This proactive approach helps identify areas where you can potentially reduce spending and improve your bottom line. Consistent monitoring also allows you to anticipate fluctuations in expenses and plan accordingly, improving the precision of your financial forecasting and tax planning. Yearly tax preparation should not be the only time you examine your records; regular reviews offer a continuous understanding of your business finances, paving the way for sustainable tax optimization.

5 Estate Planning & Trusts

Effective estate planning is crucial for minimizing your tax burden and ensuring a smooth transition of assets to your heirs. Understanding the basics of wills and trusts is the first step. A will, simply put, dictates how your assets will be distributed after your death. However, a will goes through probate, a court process that can be time-consuming and expensive. Trusts, on the other hand, offer more control and privacy, avoiding probate altogether. Different types of trusts exist, each with its unique tax implications, requiring careful consideration based on your specific financial circumstances and goals. Choosing the right trust structure is paramount for minimizing potential estate taxes and preserving your family's financial well-being. Consult with an estate planning attorney to determine which type of trust best aligns with your needs. This initial consultation will help you navigate the complexities and nuances of various trust options, enabling you to make informed decisions.

Proper estate planning extends beyond simply creating a will or trust. It's a proactive strategy that involves careful consideration of various factors like asset distribution, tax implications, and the future needs of your beneficiaries. A well-structured estate plan safeguards your assets, minimizes legal complexities, and ensures your wishes are honored after your passing. Your family's future financial security depends on effective estate planning, so don't hesitate to seek professional guidance for comprehensive planning. Failing to do so may result in unnecessary taxes, legal battles, and emotional distress for your loved ones.

Minimizing estate taxes requires a multi-faceted approach. One key strategy involves utilizing annual gift tax exclusions. The IRS allows you to gift a certain amount of money each year without incurring gift taxes. This strategy enables you to transfer assets to your heirs gradually, reducing the overall value of your estate subject to estate taxes upon your death. Additionally, strategic gifting to charities can offer significant tax deductions, lowering your taxable estate. It's advisable to consult with a tax advisor to understand your gift tax exemption limits and explore additional tax-efficient gifting strategies tailored to your individual circumstances. Careful planning of these gifts can significantly reduce future tax liabilities for your heirs.

Gifting strategies are multifaceted and require careful consideration of various tax implications. You can reduce your taxable estate significantly by gifting assets during your lifetime. This allows for tax-efficient wealth transfer, shielding your assets from estate taxes. You must be mindful of the annual gift tax exclusion and the lifetime gift tax exemption to fully understand the implications of your actions. Careful planning, along with an understanding of gift and estate tax laws, is imperative. Consider gifting appreciated assets, as doing so allows your beneficiaries to benefit from stepped-up basis rules upon your death, offering significant tax advantages. Remember to discuss with a tax professional the best strategy for your specific situation and the tax implications.

Beyond individual gifting, charitable giving offers another powerful strategy for estate tax minimization. Donating assets to qualified charities reduces the overall value of your taxable estate. This can result in substantial tax savings for your estate and provide significant benefits to your chosen charities. Different types of charitable gifts offer varied tax benefits. Outright gifts, donations of appreciated assets, and charitable remainder trusts offer distinct advantages and require consideration of your individual circumstances and goals. A financial advisor with expertise in charitable giving strategies can help you understand which approach is most suitable for you. Their expertise will ensure that you take advantage of all available tax benefits while maximizing your charitable contribution. Remember that proper planning in this field is paramount.

5.1 Will & Trust Basics

A will, simply put, is a legal document outlining your wishes for the distribution of your assets after your death. It names an executor, the person responsible for carrying out those wishes, and specifies who inherits what. Without a will, your state's intestacy laws determine the distribution, a process that may not align with your intentions and could lead to unintended tax consequences for your heirs. Consider, for example, the complexities that arise if you own significant real estate or have several beneficiaries with differing needs. A well-drafted will ensures a smoother and more efficient transfer of assets, minimizing potential family disputes and tax burdens.

Trusts, on the other hand, offer a more sophisticated approach to asset management and distribution. They act as separate legal entities, holding assets on behalf of beneficiaries. This separation provides several benefits. For example, a trust can help protect assets from creditors, reduce estate taxes, and provide for beneficiaries with special needs, perhaps ensuring that your loved ones do not experience financial hardship at the worst possible times. You also have numerous trust options, including revocable trusts and irrevocable trusts, each designed to serve different purposes and offer varied levels of control. Understanding which type of trust best suits your needs and financial situation is paramount.

The choice between a will and a trust, or even using both, depends heavily on your individual circumstances. For instance, if your estate is relatively straightforward with few assets and clear beneficiaries, a well-written will might suffice. However, for those with significant assets, complex family dynamics, or a desire for greater control over asset distribution and protection, a trust might be a more prudent choice. The specific tax advantages of each also play a crucial role in this decision-making process. Consulting with an estate planning attorney is essential to determine the optimal approach for your particular circumstances, making sure that your choices are legally sound and tax-efficient.

One key area where trusts demonstrate their value is in minimizing estate taxes. Depending on the size of your estate, these taxes can be substantial, significantly impacting the inheritance your heirs receive. Trusts provide several mechanisms for reducing or potentially eliminating these taxes. One major way this is done is by strategically structuring assets within the trust, ensuring the estate's value for tax purposes is either lowered or broken down into smaller amounts, each of which could avoid the applicable tax threshold. This complex process requires careful planning and legal expertise to maximize its effectiveness. In many cases, trusts are used as a crucial tool in the minimization process, and should always be discussed with qualified legal professionals in any tax minimization strategy.

Furthermore, trusts can offer flexibility in asset management and distribution that a simple will cannot. For example, you can establish a trust that provides for income distribution to beneficiaries over time, ensuring their financial security while preventing them from potentially squandering a large inheritance. A trust can even specify that certain assets only become available at specific life events, like graduation or marriage. It can also include specific instructions on the distribution of assets which, as previously mentioned, is not always available when a state handles inheritance. You can build in protection for vulnerable beneficiaries, and also provide protection for your estate from financial claims made after you've passed away. Such control and flexibility are invaluable, especially for those with minor children or beneficiaries with potential financial vulnerabilities.

The legal and tax implications surrounding wills and trusts are complex, requiring careful consideration and professional guidance. Seeking advice from a qualified estate planning attorney is critical. They can help you navigate the intricacies of estate planning, ensuring that your choices align with your financial goals and minimize potential tax liabilities. Remember, proactive planning is crucial. Delaying these important decisions could have significant repercussions, not only financially, but in terms of ensuring your wishes are fulfilled efficiently and fairly. Don't underestimate the importance of understanding the implications of your choices and, most importantly, doing so with the help of professionals. This careful approach will significantly improve your chances of creating a smooth transition of your estate, ensuring that your loved ones are protected and your financial legacy is handled with precision and care. This is not a process you should undertake alone; expert advice should form the base of your estate plan.

5.2 Estate Tax Minimization

Effective estate tax minimization requires proactive planning, beginning well in advance of anticipated wealth transfer. Understanding the intricacies of estate tax laws is crucial; these laws vary significantly based on jurisdiction and are subject to change, emphasizing the need for ongoing professional guidance. Don't rely solely on generalized advice; seek personalized counsel from a qualified estate planning attorney or financial advisor familiar with your specific circumstances. They can help navigate the complex landscape of tax codes and devise a tailored strategy.

A cornerstone of estate tax reduction involves strategic gifting. Gifting assets to beneficiaries during your lifetime can lessen the taxable estate's value. However, annual gift tax exclusions and lifetime gift tax exemptions exist, limiting the amount you can gift tax-free. Careful consideration of these limitations is paramount to avoid incurring unexpected tax liabilities. Remember, consulting a tax professional ensures you stay within legal boundaries while maximizing the effectiveness of your gifting strategy. This professional can help you understand the intricacies of gift tax laws, helping you plan ahead and avoid mistakes that could lead to penalties.

Properly structuring your will and establishing trusts are powerful tools in minimizing estate taxes. A well-drafted will ensures your assets are distributed according to your wishes, minimizing potential disputes among heirs. Different types of trusts, such as irrevocable life insurance trusts (ILITs) and qualified personal residence trusts (QPRTs), offer specific tax advantages. An ILIT, for instance, can help shield life insurance benefits from estate taxes. Similarly, a QPRTs can lower estate taxes on your primary residence. These trusts, however, come with their own complexities and require careful planning and legal expertise.

Beyond trusts and wills, charitable giving presents another opportunity for estate tax reduction. Donations to qualified charities can reduce your taxable estate, offering both philanthropic and tax benefits. You should explore various charitable giving vehicles, such as charitable remainder trusts (CRTs) and charitable lead trusts (CLTs). These vehicles offer unique tax advantages and allow you to support your favored causes while strategically managing your estate. Remember that careful documentation and legal counsel are essential for claiming these deductions and ensuring compliance with tax regulations.

Utilizing various investment strategies can influence your estate's overall value and consequently, the estate tax burden. Diversification across different asset classes—stocks, bonds, real estate—can help mitigate risk and potentially increase overall value, indirectly lowering your tax liability. However, careful consideration must be given to potential capital gains taxes that could arise from the sale of assets. An experienced financial advisor can help navigate these complexities, balancing growth potential with tax efficiency, ensuring that any gains are protected from heavy taxation.

Minimizing estate tax isn't just about reducing immediate tax liability; it's also about preserving your legacy for future generations. By strategically planning your estate, you can ensure that your heirs receive the maximum benefit of your hard work and accumulated wealth. Remember, estate planning is an ongoing process, requiring regular review and adjustments to accommodate changing circumstances and evolving tax laws. Proactive engagement with qualified professionals—attorneys, financial advisors, and tax specialists—is essential for creating a comprehensive and effective estate plan, allowing for a smooth transition of your assets while minimizing the potential tax burden on your heirs. Failing to plan is planning to fail; seize the opportunity to protect your legacy and secure your family's financial future.

5.3 Gifting Strategies

Gifting strategies offer a powerful method for reducing your overall tax liability and transferring wealth efficiently to future generations. Careful planning is crucial, however, as improper execution can lead to unintended tax consequences. Understanding the annual gift tax exclusion, which allows for a certain amount of gifting each year without incurring tax, is fundamental. This exclusion amount is adjusted annually for inflation, so it's essential to consult the latest IRS guidelines. Failing to do so could result in significant underestimation of your allowable gifting capacity and potentially lead to unnecessary tax burdens.

Strategic gifting can help reduce your estate tax burden later in life. By gifting assets during your lifetime, you effectively shrink your taxable estate, leaving less for estate taxes to claim upon your passing. This is particularly effective with appreciating assets, whose value increases over time, minimizing the tax on that appreciation. Think of it as a preemptive strike against the estate tax, a savvy financial maneuver that gives you control over the future tax implications of your assets. Proper estate planning, in conjunction with a robust gifting strategy, ensures a smoother transition of assets to your beneficiaries.

The choice of asset gifted significantly impacts the tax implications. Gifting highly appreciated assets, such as stocks or real estate, can lead to capital gains taxes for the recipient upon sale. However, gifting assets with a low basis might be a more tax-advantageous strategy. This complex decision requires careful consideration of your personal financial situation, your beneficiaries' circumstances and professional advice to make informed decisions. Don't overlook the potential impact on your beneficiaries' tax situations. A gift might inadvertently push them into a higher tax bracket, negating some of the intended benefits of your generous action. Therefore, thoughtful planning is key.

Careful documentation of gifts is paramount. Maintaining detailed records of all gifts, including dates, amounts, and recipients, is vital for tax compliance. This isn't merely a matter of good practice; it's a legal necessity. The IRS scrutinizes gifting activities, and inadequate record-keeping can lead to audits and penalties. These penalties can far outweigh the potential tax savings from poorly documented gifting. This meticulously organized approach is crucial to your overall tax strategy and its long-term effectiveness.

Consider utilizing trusts for more complex gifting situations. Irrevocable trusts, for instance, provide significant control over the distribution of assets and can offer significant tax advantages. However, these trusts come with their own complexities and potential legal ramifications. A qualified estate planning attorney can help navigate these complexities. It's important to remember that this specialized advice is crucial in ensuring the most effective and legally sound strategy for your individual needs. Don't consider it an unnecessary expense, but a sound investment in the future financial security of yourself and your beneficiaries.

For those with significant assets to transfer, establishing a gifting schedule can be advantageous. This involves strategically gifting smaller amounts over several years, rather than a single, large gift. This approach helps minimize the impact on any one year's gift tax liability. Remember, this method is about long-term planning, not just immediate tax relief. A well-designed plan, adjusted to reflect the fluctuations of the economy and potential legal changes, can safeguard your legacy.

Finally, always consult with qualified professionals. Tax laws are complex and frequently change. A competent tax advisor and estate planning attorney can provide personalized guidance, taking into account your individual circumstances and financial goals. This professional guidance is not an optional extra; it's a critical component of successful gifting strategies and overall tax planning. Ignoring this crucial step could negate the benefits of careful planning, costing you far more in the long run. Their expertise provides a safeguard against costly mistakes and ensures a smoother, more effective wealth transfer. Remember, securing your family's financial future requires a proactive and informed approach, guided by sound professional advice.

6 Navigating Tax Audits

A tax audit can feel like a sudden storm, threatening to disrupt your carefully constructed financial landscape. The initial shock often gives way to anxiety, but understanding the process is your first line of defense. Remember, the IRS doesn't automatically assume wrongdoing; audits often stem from random selection, mathematical discrepancies, or red flags within your return. Knowing this can significantly alleviate some of the initial stress. Proactive preparation is key. Gather all relevant documentation—tax returns, receipts, bank statements, and supporting evidence for any deductions or credits claimed. Organize these materials methodically; a well-organized system will make navigating the audit process significantly smoother and less stressful.
Maintain meticulous records. This isn't just about having the documents; it's about their clarity and accessibility. Think of it as building a case for yourself. Clear and concise documentation demonstrating the accuracy of your tax filings is your strongest ally. This careful attention to detail not only minimizes the likelihood of an audit but also significantly simplifies the process should one occur. This seemingly simple act of organization can be the difference between a quick resolution and a protracted, stressful ordeal.
Deciding whether to represent yourself or hire a professional is a crucial step. Representing yourself can save money, but it demands a thorough understanding of tax law and the ability to

present your case effectively. Consider your comfort level with tax regulations and your ability to navigate complex legal processes. If you lack confidence or expertise in these areas, engaging a qualified tax professional is a wise investment. Their experience can significantly improve your odds of a favorable outcome, potentially saving you far more than the cost of their services in the long run. They understand the intricacies of tax law and can effectively advocate for your rights, potentially mitigating penalties and interest. They also possess the knowledge and experience to negotiate with the IRS effectively.

Regardless of your choice, cooperation is critical. Respond promptly to all IRS inquiries, providing the necessary documentation in a timely manner. Avoid being evasive or dismissive; this can escalate the situation unnecessarily. A cooperative approach demonstrates your commitment to resolving the matter fairly and efficiently. Remember, the IRS operates within specific guidelines and procedures; understanding these processes and approaching the audit with respect and professionalism can drastically improve the chances of a positive resolution. Even if you believe a claim is incorrect, presenting your case calmly and rationally, backed by evidence, often yields better results than confrontation. If the audit results in a disagreement, explore all available options. This might involve providing additional documentation, presenting a well-reasoned counter-argument, or even filing a formal appeal. The appeals process can be intricate, but understanding the relevant regulations and employing sound strategy increases the likelihood of a favorable decision. Remember, persistence is key; it's not uncommon for audits to take time, and patience is crucial throughout the entire process. Don't be discouraged by initial setbacks; carefully consider every avenue to ensure a just and equitable outcome. The IRS has clear procedures for appeals, and understanding those procedures is essential for protecting your rights and presenting your case effectively. Seek professional guidance if needed; navigating this complex process is easier with the help of an experienced advocate.

6.1 Understanding Audits

An audit, while daunting, is simply a thorough examination of your tax return by the tax authorities. Think of it as a detailed review of your financial paperwork, verifying the accuracy and completeness of your reported income, deductions, and credits. It's not necessarily a sign of wrongdoing; many audits are routine, a random selection from a pool of tax returns. However, understanding the process will empower you to navigate it with confidence, minimizing stress and potential penalties.

The IRS, or your equivalent national tax authority, employs various methods to select returns for audit. Some are completely random, a lottery system designed to ensure fair and impartial review. Others target specific industries or taxpayers exhibiting unusual patterns, such as unusually high deductions compared to income. Understanding these selection methods can't prevent an audit, but knowing that they exist might alleviate some anxiety if you find yourself under scrutiny.

Preparation is key. Gathering all relevant documents before the audit begins significantly reduces stress and increases efficiency. Organize your tax returns, receipts, bank statements, and any other supporting documentation chronologically and by category. Creating a digital archive also allows for easy access and sharing of information, should the auditor require specific details. Digital organization ensures you will be able to find the information you need quickly and conveniently. Consider creating a comprehensive checklist to ensure all potentially relevant materials are included.

If you receive an audit notification, don't panic. Respond promptly and professionally, acknowledging the notice and requesting clarification if needed. Maintain detailed records of all communication with the auditor, including dates, times, and summaries of conversations. This documentation is invaluable if disagreements arise and is essential for accurate and reliable records. The better your records, the better you'll be equipped to provide responses. Furthermore, always remain respectful and cooperative throughout the process.

The audit itself might involve several meetings or correspondence exchanges. Be prepared to answer questions clearly and concisely, providing supporting documentation where applicable. If you're uncertain about an answer, it's perfectly acceptable to request clarification or time to gather additional information. Don't try to hide or downplay anything; honesty is the best policy. Remember, the goal is to demonstrate the accuracy and legality of your tax filing, not to win a contest.

Should you discover an error on your tax return, correct it immediately and submit an amended return. It's often better to self-correct, which shows initiative and cooperation, rather than having the auditor uncover the error. This proactive approach demonstrates good faith and might minimize penalties, and demonstrates a collaborative attitude towards the process. The auditor might then just recommend the correction, rather than imposing additional penalties.

While you may represent yourself, it is often advisable to seek professional assistance, particularly if the audit involves complex issues or significant financial implications. A qualified tax professional possesses the expertise to navigate the intricacies of tax law, advocate effectively on your behalf, and ensure the process adheres to all regulations and fair procedures. While a professional can add additional cost, it can also save you money and time in the long run. Consider carefully weighing the cost versus the potential implications of a negative outcome.

Navigating a tax audit can be a challenging but manageable experience. By understanding the process, preparing thoroughly, remaining calm and communicative, and seeking professional advice when necessary, you can significantly improve the outcome. Remember, the goal is not to avoid audits, which is nearly impossible, but to be fully prepared and equipped to handle them efficiently and effectively. This preparation minimizes stress and ultimately safeguards your financial well-being. Remember, audits are part of the system, and while it's frustrating, going into them calmly and strategically is beneficial.

6.2 Preparing for an Audit

A tax audit can feel like a sudden storm, threatening to disrupt your financial peace. Preparation, however, is your best defense, transforming that storm into a manageable drizzle. Begin by meticulously organizing your financial records. This isn't just about gathering tax returns; it's about compiling every document that supports your deductions and credits – receipts, bank statements, investment records, invoices, and anything else relevant to your claimed expenses. Think of it as creating a comprehensive financial autobiography, detailing every relevant financial transaction. The more organized your records are, the smoother your audit will likely proceed.

Don't underestimate the power of digital organization. Cloud-based storage offers easy access, version control, and enhanced security. Consider using specialized accounting software to categorize and track your transactions. Some platforms even generate reports that neatly summarize your financial activity, streamlining the audit process significantly. However, remember that digital organization requires regular back-ups and security measures. You would regret relying solely on a digital system and having it crash or become inaccessible during the audit.

Next, understand the types of audits you might face. A correspondence audit involves a simple request for clarification or additional documentation through written communication. A field audit is more involved, with a tax agent visiting your home or business to review your records. Knowing what to expect allows you to mentally prepare and reduces the anxiety often associated with audits. Familiarize yourself with the IRS's procedures and rights during an audit; knowledge is power, especially during a challenging situation.

Thoroughly review your tax returns from previous years. Identify any potential areas of concern or inconsistencies. This proactive approach allows you to address any discrepancies before they become major issues during an audit. It also helps you understand patterns in your tax filing to avoid future problems. It is better to rectify past mistakes and learn from them. Look for potential discrepancies in your tax returns and prepare to justify every claim, especially those with unusually large deductions or credits. Be prepared to explain every transaction, no matter how small, because they can all add up.

Furthermore, it's crucial to maintain a professional and cooperative attitude throughout the audit process. Respond promptly to all communication from the IRS. Treat the tax agent with respect, even if you feel frustrated or nervous. Your demeanor will significantly impact the course of the audit. If you don't understand something or are unsure how to answer a question, be honest and say so. Never try to hide or misrepresent information. Transparency and honesty are your best allies in navigating the audit successfully.

Finally, while you might choose to represent yourself, consider seeking professional help. A tax attorney or enrolled agent possesses specialized knowledge and experience in handling tax audits. They can provide invaluable guidance, ensuring your rights are protected, and advocate on your behalf, significantly reducing stress and improving your chances of a favorable outcome. However, remember to thoroughly vet any professional you consider engaging to ensure their qualifications and reputation meet your expectations and that you are completely comfortable with their approach. The cost of professional representation might be worth the peace of mind. Ultimately, thorough preparation is your best weapon against the anxieties and uncertainties of a tax audit.

6.3 Representing Yourself

Facing a tax audit can be daunting, but understanding your rights and responsibilities is crucial. The IRS generally prefers correspondence, beginning with a notice or letter explaining the discrepancy. Responding promptly and professionally is key; ignoring them won't make them disappear. Your initial response should acknowledge the notice, state your intention to cooperate, and request clarification on any points you don't understand. Don't admit guilt if you're unsure. Gathering all relevant documentation, including tax returns, receipts, bank statements, and supporting evidence for any deductions or credits claimed, is vital. Organizing these meticulously makes the process significantly smoother. Remember, detailed record-keeping is your best defense.

If you decide to represent yourself, remember clarity and conciseness are your allies. Prepare a clear, organized presentation of your case, emphasizing the accuracy of your tax filings. Use plain language, avoiding jargon, ensuring the auditor comprehends your points without difficulty. Be respectful, even if frustrated; maintaining a professional demeanor is essential for a positive outcome. A calm and collected approach increases your chances of a favorable resolution. Present evidence methodically, connecting each piece of evidence to the specific point it supports. Anticipate potential questions the auditor might have and prepare concise answers. If you are unsure about something, be honest and state so; claiming knowledge you don't have could backfire.

However, representing yourself doesn't mean going it alone. Seek guidance from reputable resources. The IRS website provides numerous publications and instructions, offering valuable insights into the audit process. Tax law is complex, and free resources from the IRS or trusted non-profit organizations can help demystify the process. They can guide you through navigating the specific requirements for your case. Remember, while self-representation saves you the cost of professional fees, it demands substantial time and effort. Thorough preparation is paramount to ensure a positive outcome. Understanding the potential consequences of inaccuracies in your filings is vital; minor mistakes can escalate into serious problems if left unaddressed.

Consider the complexity of your case. A simple issue, such as a minor mathematical error, is far different from a complex dispute involving significant tax liabilities or business transactions. If you're facing complex issues, extensive documentation, or significant financial implications, seeking professional help becomes increasingly crucial. The time commitment involved in handling a complex audit, combined with the penalties for mistakes, might outweigh the cost of professional assistance. Remember, the IRS agents are trained professionals; they'll spot inconsistencies or weak points in your arguments. A tax professional can provide the expertise and experience necessary to navigate these complexities effectively. Your personal time is valuable; a qualified professional is likely to resolve the matter quicker, lessening the stress and uncertainty.

While representing yourself can be empowering and cost-effective for straightforward audits, it's critical to weigh the pros and cons based on your specific circumstances. Understanding the intricacies of tax law, gathering and presenting evidence effectively, and maintaining composure under pressure are challenging, even for experienced professionals. If you're uncertain about your ability to handle the complexities, it's wise to seek professional assistance. In many cases, it may be a more cost-effective solution in the long run. Remember, the goal is to resolve the issue fairly and efficiently, and sometimes that means acknowledging your limitations and seeking help. Don't hesitate to seek advice—it's a sign of intelligence, not weakness. The outcome is more important than personal pride.

6.4 Hiring Tax Professionals

Choosing the right tax professional is crucial, especially when facing a complex audit. It's not just about finding someone with a license; you need someone who understands your specific situation and can advocate effectively on your behalf. Look for someone with experience handling cases similar to yours, whether it's a business audit involving intricate deductions or a personal audit with significant assets. Don't hesitate to ask about their success rate in resolving disputes – a strong track record speaks volumes. Remember, this is an investment in protecting your financial future, not just an expense.

Their expertise extends beyond simple tax preparation. A seasoned tax professional can unravel the complexities of tax law, identify potential loopholes (legal ones, of course!), and strategically plan your tax future. They possess a deep understanding of the IRS's procedures and expectations, which is invaluable during an audit. A good professional will not just react to problems; they'll proactively help you structure your finances to minimize your tax burden, often through strategies that go far beyond simple deductions. Consider it as preventative medicine for your financial health.

When interviewing potential professionals, don't be afraid to ask detailed questions. Inquire about their experience with your specific type of business or financial situation. Find out about their fee structure; some charge hourly rates, while others offer flat fees, depending on the complexity of the case. Transparency about fees is key. Don't be shy; clarify any uncertainties, and always ensure that you are comfortable with the agreed-upon scope of work and the payment terms before signing any contract. This professional is your partner in navigating this critical juncture.

Furthermore, check their professional credentials and affiliations. A Certified Public Accountant (CPA) designation signifies a high level of expertise and adherence to ethical standards. Membership in professional organizations like the National Association of Tax Professionals (NATP) demonstrates a commitment to continuing education and staying abreast of evolving tax laws. This means you're dealing with someone who consistently updates their knowledge, offering you the best possible advice based on the latest regulations and rulings. Doing your homework here ensures you're working with someone who truly understands their field.

Beyond credentials, consider their communication style and responsiveness. Can you easily reach them when you have questions or concerns? Do they explain complex tax issues in a clear, understandable manner? Effective communication is essential during a stressful audit. You need someone who can not only handle the technical aspects of your case but also provide consistent, reassuring updates and clear explanations of the processes involved. Clear communication is a critical component of a successful outcome.

References are invaluable. Don't hesitate to ask for referrals from trusted sources, including financial advisors, attorneys, or other business professionals. Speaking to someone who has personally benefited from their services provides invaluable insight into the professional's capabilities and work ethic. Getting a second opinion, even after you have selected a tax professional, can be beneficial. A second pair of eyes, perhaps from another accountant or financial expert, can offer valuable insights.

Ultimately, the best tax professional for you is one who understands your unique needs and goals. Choosing the right professional is an investment in your financial well-being, reducing stress and ensuring you navigate tax challenges effectively. Therefore, take your time, gather information, and don't rush the decision-making process. This process is crucial for your peace of mind and long-term financial security. Consider it a proactive measure; prevention is always better than cure. Remember, this is not just about winning an audit; it's about establishing a long-term relationship built on trust and expertise to help you navigate your tax obligations for years to come.

6.5 Dispute Resolution

Disputes with the Internal Revenue Service (IRS) can be daunting, but understanding the process can significantly improve your chances of a favorable outcome. The IRS utilizes various methods for collecting taxes, from notices and levies to liens and even criminal prosecution. Knowing your rights and the available dispute resolution options is crucial. Remember, timely action is vital; ignoring IRS correspondence will only worsen your situation. Promptly responding to notices, providing accurate information, and documenting all communication are fundamental steps in effective dispute resolution.

Negotiation is often the first step. This may involve offering a payment plan, proposing a compromise, or presenting evidence to support your position. Clear, concise communication, supported by solid documentation, such as receipts, bank statements, and tax returns, is key. Remember, maintaining a professional and respectful tone throughout the process is essential. It will help improve your chances of reaching a mutually agreeable solution. If the IRS remains unyielding during initial negotiations, exploring alternative channels might be necessary.

The IRS offers several formal dispute resolution options. The most common is the Offer in Compromise (OIC) program, which allows taxpayers to settle their tax debt for a significantly reduced amount. Eligibility depends on several factors, including your ability to pay, income, expenses, and asset equity. Preparing a thorough and accurate OIC application is paramount; inaccuracies can lead to rejection. Seeking professional assistance from an enrolled agent or tax attorney is often advisable, particularly for complex cases. They can guide you through the process and significantly enhance your chances of success.

Appeals are another avenue for dispute resolution. If you disagree with the IRS's assessment of your tax liability, you can file an appeal through the IRS Appeals Office. This involves presenting your case to an appeals officer, who will review the evidence and potentially reverse or modify the IRS's decision. A strong appeal requires meticulous preparation. Gather all relevant documentation, including tax returns, supporting records, and expert opinions if necessary. An appeal should meticulously present your case, addressing each point of contention clearly and concisely. It's wise to seek professional assistance in preparing and presenting your appeal.

For more complex or high-stakes disputes, consider litigation in the Tax Court, District Court, or the Court of Federal Claims. Litigation is often a last resort, typically reserved for significant tax disputes or where other resolution methods have failed. Filing a lawsuit against the IRS involves substantial legal procedures, costs, and complexities. It will necessitate working with a tax attorney or law firm specializing in tax litigation. It is of paramount importance to ensure your legal representation is experienced in navigating the intricacies of the tax court system. Thorough preparation is crucial, requiring detailed documentation and a clearly defined legal strategy.

Preventing disputes is the best strategy. Maintain meticulous financial records, file your taxes accurately and on time, and seek professional assistance when needed. Investing in proper tax planning can minimize the risk of future disputes. Proactive measures, such as understanding tax laws and using available tax-planning tools, can dramatically reduce the likelihood of an audit and its consequent disputes. Regularly reviewing your tax situation and seeking professional guidance can help prevent future issues. Remember, preventative actions are far more cost-effective than resolving disputes after they arise. A proactive approach helps to ensure your long-term tax compliance and financial peace of mind.

Ultimately, resolving a tax dispute requires a multifaceted approach combining knowledge, preparation, and potentially professional assistance. While understanding your rights and the available options is crucial, proactive tax planning is your best defense. Remember, prompt action, thorough documentation, and clear communication are vital components in navigating tax disputes effectively. By following these steps and seeking professional help when necessary, you can significantly improve your chances of a favorable resolution. Navigating tax disputes successfully demands a strategic approach blending knowledge, preparation, and potentially professional assistance. This proactive approach is more effective than reactive measures, saving you time, money, and stress in the long run. The information given should not be considered professional legal or financial advice; seek assistance from a professional.

7 Long-Term Tax Planning

Predicting the future is impossible, yet anticipating potential tax law changes is crucial for long-term financial health. Consider the current political climate, economic trends, and demographic shifts; these all influence tax policy. For example, a growing national debt might lead to higher taxes across the board, affecting your income tax brackets, capital gains taxes, and estate taxes. Staying informed through reputable financial news sources, tax publications, and professional advisors is essential. Don't rely solely on social media or anecdotal evidence. Engage with professionals who specialize in tax law; they can provide insightful analysis and help you understand emerging trends. Remember, proactive planning always beats reactive problem-solving.

Regular review and adjustment of your tax plan are paramount. Your financial situation isn't static; it evolves with your career progression, family changes, and investment decisions. Annual tax planning isn't enough. A comprehensive review should be conducted at least every three to five years, or more frequently during periods of significant life changes. This review isn't just about updating your tax returns; it involves re-evaluating your overall financial strategy. Are your investments still aligned with your long-term goals? Have your risk tolerance and investment objectives shifted? Have you experienced any major life events that impact your tax situation, such as marriage, divorce, birth of a child, inheritance, or a substantial career change? Addressing these questions proactively ensures your tax plan remains relevant and effective.

Let's focus on practical steps. Begin by gathering all relevant financial documents—tax returns, investment statements, insurance policies, and estate planning documents. Thoroughly review these documents, identifying key areas that may need adjustment. Compare your current tax plan with your long-term financial goals. Are you on track to achieve your objectives, such as retirement security or wealth transfer to heirs? If not, identify the areas requiring modifications. This could involve adjustments to your investment portfolio, changes in your retirement savings contributions, or modifications to your estate planning documents. This detailed review requires patience and attention to detail; don't rush the process. Seek professional help if needed; an expert can provide unbiased insights.

The process of adjusting your tax plan might involve diversifying your investment portfolio to reduce your tax liability. For example, consider shifting a portion of your investments to tax-advantaged accounts such as 401(k)s, Roth IRAs, or health savings accounts (HSAs). These accounts offer significant tax benefits, helping reduce your current tax burden and potentially lower your future tax liability. Depending on your circumstances, explore alternative investment strategies, such as real estate or private equity, which offer potential tax advantages. Always remember, the choices you make today will have significant implications for your future tax liability. Therefore, it's critical to make informed decisions based on accurate information and expert advice.

Finally, don't underestimate the power of ongoing education. The tax landscape is constantly changing, making continuous learning essential. Attend tax seminars, workshops, or webinars to stay informed about recent tax law changes and new strategies. Subscribe to reputable tax publications and newsletters. Regularly consult with tax professionals to discuss your financial situation and obtain personalized advice. Don't consider this a one-time process; tax planning is an ongoing journey requiring vigilance, adaptation, and professional guidance. Think of it as a continuous flight plan, regularly updated and adjusted to ensure a smooth and successful tax-efficient journey. It's not just about minimizing your current tax burden, it's about securing your financial future. This proactive approach will yield significant long-term benefits, ensuring you stay ahead of the curve and secure your financial freedom for years to come. Remember, the goal is not simply to minimize your tax liability in the present, but to craft a tax strategy that ensures long-term financial stability and success.

7.1 Future Tax Changes

Predicting future tax changes is inherently uncertain; however, by analyzing current trends and proposed legislation, we can anticipate potential shifts. One area likely to see adjustments is the tax treatment of capital gains. Increased pressure on income inequality could lead to higher rates for high-income earners, or perhaps expanded brackets encompassing a wider range of income levels. This necessitates a proactive approach to investment planning, potentially shifting strategies to favor assets with lower tax burdens in the long run. Careful consideration of long-term growth versus short-term gains will become ever more critical, requiring a deeper understanding of your individual risk tolerance and financial goals.

The expanding use of technology and the gig economy may also prompt legislative changes. Currently, the taxation of remote work and freelance income can be complex, often leading to inconsistencies in reporting and liability. Expect greater clarity and possibly stricter enforcement in this sector, demanding meticulous record-keeping and a thorough understanding of self-employment tax regulations. Those operating in these realms must stay updated on relevant laws, possibly consulting with tax professionals to ensure compliance. Proactive planning, including setting aside funds for potential tax liabilities, is vital for navigating this evolving tax landscape.

Another area ripe for change involves deductions and credits. While specific programs are always subject to alteration, the overall trend suggests a potential tightening of eligibility criteria for certain deductions. This necessitates a thorough understanding of current guidelines and a proactive approach to identifying potentially vulnerable aspects of your tax strategy. Regular reviews with a tax advisor can offer insights and help you adapt your approach to remain within compliance and maximize your potential savings. Don't rely solely on past practices; anticipate adjustments and plan accordingly to mitigate any potential negative impact.

Retirement savings strategies might also see adjustments. While tax-advantaged retirement accounts remain a cornerstone of financial planning, alterations to contribution limits, distribution rules, or even the tax treatment of withdrawals are possible. Staying informed about proposed changes is crucial. Consider diversifying retirement savings across multiple accounts to minimize potential risks associated with any single account type. Regularly assess your retirement strategy's alignment with your financial goals and anticipated tax regulations, making necessary adjustments to ensure long-term financial security.

Furthermore, estate planning and inheritance taxes could undergo reform. Changes could include adjustments to exemption thresholds or the tax rates themselves, potentially impacting the strategies used for transferring wealth to heirs. Careful review of your estate plan, considering the potential implications of future legislative changes, is paramount. Consult with an estate planning attorney to ensure that your plan remains relevant and effective. Exploring options like trusts and charitable giving could offer strategic advantages in mitigating potential estate tax burdens.

Ultimately, the precise nature and timing of future tax changes remain uncertain. However, a proactive approach to financial planning is always the best defense. This includes staying informed on current tax policies and potential legislative changes, maintaining meticulous records, and regularly consulting with tax and financial professionals. Building a strong foundation of financial literacy is crucial for effectively navigating the complexities of the tax system. Treat tax planning as an ongoing process that requires constant monitoring and adjustment, adapting to the ever-shifting landscape. By staying informed and adaptable, you can better position yourself to minimize your tax burden and protect your financial future. Remember, proactive planning is key to navigating future uncertainties.

7.2 Review & Adjustment

The tax landscape is dynamic; laws change, your circumstances evolve. Therefore, a static tax plan is a recipe for inefficiency, possibly even penalties. Regular review and adjustment aren't optional – they're essential for maintaining optimal tax efficiency. Think of your tax strategy as a living document, constantly adapting to your changing financial reality.

Consider your income. Has it increased significantly? Did you experience a major life event, like marriage, divorce, the birth of a child, or a substantial inheritance? Each alters your tax bracket and potentially your eligibility for specific deductions or credits. Failing to account for these shifts could mean leaving money on the table – a costly oversight.

Let's examine deductions. Did you make significant charitable contributions this year? Have you meticulously tracked all eligible business expenses if self-employed? Reviewing your records thoroughly is crucial. Even small, overlooked deductions can cumulatively make a considerable difference. Don't underestimate the power of detailed record-keeping; it's your best defense against an audit and your strongest ally in maximizing deductions.

Investment portfolios also require periodic checks. Did your investment strategy yield capital gains? Understanding the tax implications of these gains is paramount, especially if you haven't diversified your portfolio as recommended earlier. Tax-loss harvesting, a strategy that uses losses to offset gains, might be a viable option to consider, depending on your specific portfolio. Consult with a financial advisor to ensure you align your investment strategy with your overall tax goals.

Business owners should pay particularly close attention to expense management. Are you meticulously tracking all business-related expenses? Are you leveraging all available deductions, such as home office deductions or qualified business income deductions (QBI)? These deductions offer substantial tax savings; failing to claim them represents a missed opportunity. Reviewing your business structure is also worthwhile. Is your current setup still the most tax-efficient for your evolving business needs? Consider consulting with a tax professional to explore alternative structures and optimize your tax position.

Estate planning isn't a one-time event; it requires ongoing review and adaptation. Significant changes in asset value, family dynamics, or even changes in tax laws might necessitate revisions to your will or trust. Regularly reviewing your estate plan ensures your wishes are reflected accurately, minimizing potential estate taxes and securing a smooth transition of assets to your beneficiaries. This proactive approach mitigates potential future complications for your loved ones.

Finally, staying informed is vital. Tax laws are frequently updated. Make it a habit to periodically review changes to tax legislation, understanding their potential impact on your personal tax situation. Subscription to reputable financial news sources, consultation with a tax advisor, or attendance at tax-related seminars can provide invaluable insights into potential future tax changes and how to best adapt to them. Remember, staying abreast of changes keeps you ahead of the curve. Proactive adaptation is the key to long-term tax efficiency, minimizing your tax burden consistently.

Proactive tax planning is an ongoing process; periodic reviews and adjustments are critical for success. It's not about finding loopholes; it's about intelligent, legal strategies to minimize your tax liability and maximize your financial resources.

www.ingramcontent.com/pod-product-compliance
Lightning Source LLC
LaVergne TN
LVHW022025200926
848481LV00007B/2540

9798348595579